59886126

SPORTS SCIENCE

SCIENCE 24/7

ANIMAL SCIENCE

CAR SCIENCE

COMPUTER SCIENCE

ENVIRONMENTAL SCIENCE

FASHION SCIENCE

FOOD SCIENCE

HEALTH SCIENCE

MUSIC SCIENCE

PHOTO SCIENCE

SPORTS SCIENCE

TRAVEL SCIENCE

SCIENCE 24/7

SPORTS SCIENCE

JANE P. GARDNER

SCIENCE CONSULTANT:
RUSS LEWIN
SCIENCE AND MATH EDUCATOR

Mason Crest

Mason Crest
450 Parkway Drive, Suite D
Broomall, PA 19008
www.masoncrest.com

Printed and bound in the United States of America.

Series ISBN: 978-1-4222-3404-4
Hardback ISBN: 978-1-4222-3414-3
EBook ISBN: 978-1-4222-8498-8

First printing
1 3 5 7 9 8 6 4 2

Produced by Shoreline Publishing Group LLC
Santa Barbara, California
www.shorelinepublishing.com
Cover Photograph: Dreamstime.com/Monkey Business Images

Library of Congress Cataloging-in-Publication Data
Gardner, Jane P., author.
    Sports science / by Jane P. Gardner ; science consultant, Russ Lewin, science department chairman, Santa Barbara Middle School.
        pages cm. -- (Science 24/7)
        Audience: Ages 12+
        Audience: Grades 7 to 8.
        Includes bibliographical references and index.
ISBN 978-1-4222-3414-3 (hardback) -- ISBN 978-1-4222-3404-4 (series) -- ISBN 978-1-4222-8498-8 (ebook) 1.
Sports sciences--Juvenile literature. 2. Sports--Technological innovations--Juvenile literature. I. Title.
GV558.G37 2015
796--dc23
                                    2015014799

IMPORTANT NOTICE
The science experiments, activities, and information described in this publication are for educational use only. The publisher is not responsible for any direct, indirect, incidental or consequential damages as a result of the uses or misuses of the techniques and information within.

Contents

KEY ICONS TO LOOK FOR

Words to Understand: These words with their easy-to-understand definitions will increase the reader's understanding of the text, while building vocabulary skills.

Sidebars: This boxed material within the main text allows readers to build knowledge, gain insights, explore possibilities, and broaden their perspectives by weaving together additional information to provide realistic and holistic perspectives.

Series Glossary of Key Terms: This back-of-the-book glossary contains terminology used throughout this series. Words found here increase the reader's ability to read and comprehend higher-level books and articles in this field.

INTRODUCTION

Science. Ugh! Is this the class you have to sit through in order to get to the cafeteria for lunch? Or, yeah! This is my favorite class! Whether you look forward to science or dread it, you can't escape it. Science is all around us all the time.

What do you think of when you think about science? People in lab coats peering anxiously through microscopes while scribbling notes? Giant telescopes scanning the universe for signs of life? Submersibles trolling the dark, cold, and lonely world of the deepest ocean? Yes, these are all science and things that scientists do to learn more about our planet, outer space, and the human body. But we are all scientists. Even you.

Science is about asking questions. Why do I have to eat my vegetables? Why does the sun set in the west? Why do cats purr and dogs bark? Why am I warmer when I wear a black jacket than when I wear a white one? These are all great questions. And these questions can be the start of something big . . . the start of scientific discovery.

1. **Observe:** Ask questions. What do you see in the world around you that you don't understand? What do you wish you knew more about? Remember, there is always more than one solution to a problem. This is the starting point for scientists—and it can be the starting point for you, too!

Enrique took a slice of bread out of the package and discovered there was mold on it. "Again?" he complained. "This is the second time this all-natural bread I bought turned moldy before I could finish it. I wonder why."

2. **Research:** Find out what you can about the observation you have made. The more information you learn about your observation, the better you will understand which questions really need to be answered.

Enrique researched the term "all-natural" as it applied to his bread. He discovered that it meant that no preservatives were used. Some breads contain preservatives, which are used to "maintain freshness." Enrique wondered if it was the lack of preservatives that was allowing his bread to grow mold.

3. **Predict:** Consider what might happen if you were to design an experiment based on your research. What do you think you would find?

Enrique thought that maybe it was the lack of preservatives in his bread that was causing the mold. He predicted that bread containing preservatives would last longer than "all-natural" breads.

4. **Develop a Hypothesis:** A hypothesis is a possible answer or solution to a scientific problem. Sometimes, they are written as an "if-then" statement. For example, "If I get a good night's sleep, then I will do well on the test tomorrow." This is not a fact; there is no guarantee that the hypothesis is correct. But it is a statement that can be tested with an experiment. And then, if necessary, revised once the experiment has been done.

Enrique thinks that he knows what is going on. He figures that the preservatives in the bread are what keeps it from getting moldy. His working hypothesis is, "If bread contains preservatives, it will not grow mold." He is now ready to test his hypothesis.

5. **Design an Experiment:** An experiment is designed to test a hypothesis. It is important when designing an experiment to look at all the variables. Variables are the factors that will change in the experiment. Some variables will be independent—these won't change. Others are dependent and will change as the experiment progresses. A control is necessary, too. This is a constant throughout the experiment against which results can be compared.

Enrique plans his experiment. He chooses two slices of his bread, and two slices of the bread with preservatives. He uses a small kitchen scale to ensure that the slices are approximately the same weight. He places a slice of each on the windowsill where they will receive the same amount of sunlight. He places the other two slices in a dark cupboard. He checks on his bread every day for a week. He finds that his bread gets mold in both places while the bread with preservatives starts to grow a little mold in the sunshine but none in the cupboard.

6. **Revise the hypothesis:** Sometimes the result of your experiment will show that the original hypothesis is incorrect. That is okay! Science is all about taking risks, making mistakes, and learning from them. Rewriting a hypothesis after examining the data is what this is all about.

Enrique realized it may be more than the preservatives that prevents mold. Keeping the bread out of the sunlight and in a dark place will help preserve it, even without preservatives. He has decided to buy smaller quantities of bread now, and keep it in the cupboard.

This book has activities for you to try at the end of each chapter. They are meant to be fun, and teach you a little bit at the same time. Sometimes, you'll be asked to design your own experiment. Think back to Enrique's experience when you start designing your own. And remember—science is about being curious, being patient, and not being afraid of saying you made a mistake. There are always other experiments to be done!

1
TRAINING TABLE 101

Buck and Gordo staked out a table at the food court. It was lunchtime and they were preparing to dig into massive meals. With the table secured, they eyed the choices. All around them was a buffet of burgers, pizza, fries, Chinese food, sandwiches, and more. Gordo took a careful look around and then made a beeline for the hamburger stand.

"Double-double with cheese, plus fries animal-style, please," Gordo said gleefully. Animal-style meant adding chili and cheese to the fries.

"Dude, you're going to choke on that," said Buck. "And you've got a game later today. What are you thinking?"

Gordo eyed his friend, who was not a stud high school football player like he was. "Buck, I gotta feed the machine, you know. This all-star body needs a lot of calories to keep the engine running."

"So you know more than players in the NFL know about eating, do you?" answered Buck, who was indeed not a star athlete, but who knew a lot more about fitness and science than his friend.

"Well, I don't know what they know, but I know what I like," Gordo retorted.

"You look up to them when they play and you copy their moves on the field," Buck continued. "You should copy what a lot of them do off the field, too. I just read a long article about how NFL players, and in fact players in most pro sports, are paying a lot more attention to what they eat these days."

"C'mon," Gordo answered, eyeing the tray of food that had just landed in front of him. "You're telling me that a big offensive lineman wouldn't just love to dive into this pile of greasy delight?"

"Of course he would," said Buck. "But that's the point. To make the right choices in nutrition, whether you're a pro athlete, a high school player like you, or even someone who is not an athlete—"

"Like you, skinny!" Gordo interrupted.

"Yes, like me, loudmouth," Buck said. "But it's still true. The guys in the NFL don't wolf down greasy, fatty meals anymore. They focus on choosing lean protein instead of fatty stuff. They pile on the greens and the fruits. When they eat bread, they try to choose whole grain styles. All that adds up to players being able to stay stronger for longer."

Buck stopped off and picked up a salad with grilled chicken at the next stand.

"How can you eat that?" Gordo said, shaking his head.

"I think it actually tastes pretty good," Buck said. "And it makes me feel better to make a choice that will help me stay strong."

They returned to the table and started to eat.

Through a mouthful of food, Gordo mumbled, "How do those guys in the NFL know what to eat? Is that something they learn in training camp?"

"Actually, they have probably been learning about it for years. At the top levels of college athletics, coaches and schools are paying more and more attention to the science of nutrition. When players go to the athletic dining hall to eat their meals, they might have cards spelling out a good meal

Words to Understand

lean in terms of meat, describing cuts that are low in fat, either because of the animal or the amount of fat in the cut

nutritionist a medical professional who focuses on providing information to patients on the right foods for them to eat, based on their needs

plan or posters pointing out which foods meet which requirements. At the pro level, a team **nutritionist** is usually around to give advice, too."

"Oh, well, then that's my excuse. We don't have a team nutritionist," Gordo said, sauce dripping from his chin.

"You don't need to have someone standing over you watching what you eat, Gordo. You know that choices like you made today aren't the best ones. You're thinking with your mouth, not your head."

"Well, my mouth is very happy right now," Gordo said, but he was getting the sinking feeling that his friend was right. In just a few hours, he'd be taking the field for his high school . . . and he was worried that he might be feeling every one of those fries as he tried to keep up with the other team. *I hope they didn't have lean chicken and a salad before the game,* he thought.

For a while, 275-pound (125-kg) first baseman Prince Fielder said he followed a vegetarian diet.

One Big Menu

The days of NFL players stepping up to the training-camp buffet and loading up on greasy food are over. Today's NFL players know that good nutrition can turn into better play . . . and more money. Still, they are big guys and can put away a lot of food. Philly.com reported that at one dinner, the Philadelphia Eagles put away 250 pounds (113.6 kg) each of filet mignon and lobster tails. A typical breakfast might include 70 pounds (31.7 kg) of eggs and 30 pounds (13.7 kg) of bacon. To help players with their options, the nutrition staff puts stickers on the food choices: green means low fat, yellow means medium, and red is for high fat foods. Even when eating meat, NFL players know that lean protein will give them the strength they need without adding pounds.

Try It Yourself

Make your own "training table" menu. See if you can create a list of meals for a long weekend of hard work at training camp. Try to create meals that follow the myplate.gov diagram below. The diagram shows how much of each kind of food you should eat each day. Look up recipes online and check ingredients. Can you build menus that are worth 3,000 calories each day? Try to make a breakfast, lunch, snack, and dinner that fill the grid. It's okay to choose meals that you'd like to try yourself, but make sure to add some food challenges, too. Trying some new things (including vegetables!) won't hurt!

Materials:

- paper and pencil
- poster board
- Internet access
- cookbooks (check your pantry; your family probably has some)

1. Make a grid on the poster board that shows four food sections for each of three days: Friday, Saturday, and Sunday.

2. Make notes on what you know you like to eat and research some calorie counts. If you can note sugar content, that's even better to know. Make sure to include protein in each meal (except maybe the snacks).

3. Can you keep carbohydrates down? Can you keep protein up? Can you find a variety of vegetables?

There is no right answer to this activity; it's an exercise to make you think more about what you eat and how it affects your body. Making plans like this is a lifelong activity! Why not start now?

2
PHYSICS
IN FIRST PLACE

After cleaning up their lunch trays, Buck and Gordo had some time before they had to get back to school so Gordo could get ready for the game that night. As always, Buck would be in the stands rooting for his friend.

They decided to poke around the sporting goods store. There were always new things to try on and Buck actually needed some new running clothes.

As they walked into the store, there was a huge display of soccer balls, soccer clothes, and soccer shoes. Above the display was a series of posters of famous current and former players. While Buck looked at them, impressed by their skills and abilities, Gordo did not agree.

"Soccer is boring," he said. "They just run around in their shorts and kick the ball."

"Well, the rest of the world does not agree with you, dude," Buck said. "And some of those guys can do a lot more than just kick the ball. They can make it perform magic."

"What do you mean, magic?" Gordo asked.

"The way soccer players can make a ball bend in flight can seem like magic," Buck said. He pointed to one of the posters that showed David Beckham about to strike the ball with his right foot.

"After Beckham hits that ball, it will curve around a wall of players standing ten yards away from him," Buck said. "By hitting it just the right way, he'll take advantage of physics to get the ball into the goal."

"Physics? I thought you said it was magic," Gordo laughed.

"Well, to we mere mortals, it seems like magic, but what Beckham and other players do to make balls curve is based on science. I learned in physics class about the Magnus effect. When force is applied to a sphere—that's a ball shape, knucklehead—so that it rotates, the rotation creates higher pressure on one side of the ball. That pressure forces the ball to curve in a direction away from that force. So as it moves forward spinning, the force also makes it curve.

"The magic is how Beckham can put that much spin on a ball with enough force and direction to make it curve to where he wants. He combined the **Magnus effect** with a magical one to create goal after goal."

"And then he took his shirt off and ran down the field, right?" laughed Gordo.

"Laugh all you want, pigskin head, but that ability made Beckham one of the richest athletes on the planet. Just to make you even crazier, though, there is also math involved. Some scientists in England worked out a formula that can actually help determine the amount of bend if you know **variables** such as **velocity**, density of the air, and distance of the kick."

He grabbed a ball from the display and put it on the ground.

"Let me show you," Buck said. "I'm no expert, and there's not enough room in here to actually kick the ball, but these are the basics. As Beckham or another player aiming to curve strikes the ball, they do it from the outside, reaching across the ball to strike it. They pull their foot across the ball instead of straight ahead. This creates the spin that is needed for the Magnus effect to come into play. The more spin, the more

Magnus effect the reaction of air pressure around a moving, spinnning sphere that reduces the pressure on one side of the sphere, causing it to alter course

variables individual pieces of data or information that can change depending on when they are observed or recorded or if conditions change

velocity a measurement of the speed of an object moving through space

curve. The more power, the more curve and the farther it goes. It's physics, but it takes years of practice to perfect."

"So what about a curveball in baseball," Gordo asked. "Is it the same deal? At least that's a sport I can understand!"

"That's about the same thing," Buck said. "Instead of putting on spin with his foot, the pitcher puts spin on the ball with his hand, wrist, and arm . . . the way he throws it. The faster the spin, the more the pressure lowers and the more the effect takes place. Softball pitchers can do it, too."

"Okay, that's all pretty cool," Gordo said. "But what about a real sport. You won't see any curved footballs in our game today."

"Ah, but physics will play a big part in that," Buck said. He led him over to another display . . . and another lesson.

Another Curving Pioneer

The great soccer player David Beckham was not the first to curve a ball around a wall or a defender. No one really knows who invented this kind of kick; Beckham was just the one that made it famous. In baseball, a curveball is a pitch thrown by the pitcher. Baseball legend says that one player did invent it. In the 1860s, righthander Candy Cummings (inset from Baseball Hall of Fame) was slinging some clam shells on a beach. He saw how the curved clam shell swerved when he threw it a certain way. He wondered if the same would happen to the spherical baseball. After some experimenting, he made it happen. At first, people thought it was an optical illusion. But by bending a pitch around a fixed object, Cummings showed that the ball did change its path. Batters since have cursed that discovery!

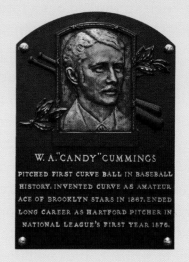

W. A. "CANDY" CUMMINGS

PITCHED FIRST CURVE BALL IN BASEBALL
HISTORY. INVENTED CURVE AS AMATEUR
ACE OF BROOKLYN STARS IN 1867. ENDED
LONG CAREER AS HARTFORD PITCHER IN
NATIONAL LEAGUE'S FIRST YEAR 1876.

Try It Yourself

See if you can make a soccer ball curve. Although this might take a few tries to get right, you'll not only see physics in action, but get a little exercise as well!

Materials:
- soccer ball
- an open space to kick
- 3-4 cones or stakes

1. Place the cones or stakes so that they line up about 10 yards apart.

2. Place the soccer ball another 10 yards beyond the cone at one end of the line.

3. First, kick the ball with the inside of your foot and try to hit the first cone. Try to make the ball roll or fly straight, not in a curve. The best way to do this is hit the ball with the kicking foot at a right angle to the non-kicking foot. Approach the ball from directly behind it in line with the cone. Think of the letter L.

4. Now see if you can curve it around the first cone and hit the second cone. To make a ball curve, strike the ball with the inside of your foot, but approach it from the side, not directly behind it. Think 45-degree angle.

5. Practice until you can make the ball move in an arc. Now experiment with other curves. Can you kick it farther to hit the third cone in the line? Does the curve have to be wider or less sharp for that kick?

6. For real experts, place the ball closer to the first cone and try to create a curve that goes past it and hits or goes near a far cone. What changes did you have to make to your kick or how you hit the ball to accomplish this?

3
ON TARGET

Gordo happily grabbed a football from the bin. His hand automatically covered part of the laces as he held it like a quarterback about to make a pass.

"Go long!" he shouted to Buck.

"Well, there's not very much room to go long here, but I see that you're already using science as you hold the ball."

"Hey, wait a minute," Gordo said. "This is just how I hold the ball. I didn't learn it in science class!"

Buck laughed and said, "Well, no matter where you learned it, that grip is the first part of the science of how a football moves forward while rotating in a spiral motion."

"Well, sure, everyone knows that the best way to throw a football is with a spiral," Gordo said, happy to be back on a topic where he was comfortable. "It makes the ball go straighter and faster. The last thing you want to try to catch is a wobbly pass. You know what we call that, don't you?"

"No," Buck said, happy to let his friend show off.

"A wounded duck! A football pass that doesn't come out with a true spiral looks like some poor bird with an injured wing."

"Okay, but why does a spiral work better, did you ever wonder that?" Buck asked.

"Of course not," Gordo said, spinning the ball into the air over his head.

"Well, it will not surprise you to learn that many people have wondered that, and physics gives us the answers. It starts with that grip, as you so kindly demonstrated. By holding the ball on the laces, on the side, that is, rather than the point, when the ball is thrown it rolls off the fingers. That creates a spin pattern around the widest diameter of the ball.

"And that spin is what makes the ball go straight. Physicists call it gyroscopic torque. That's a fancy term for the fact that the spin is perpendicular, or at right angles, to the length of the ball. In a perfect spiral, the forward force from the passer matches the spiral torque of the spin to create a spot-on pass."

"Okay, you've now officially made football boring. I did not think that was possible. Man, what are you talking about? Can't you just enjoy a nice, crisp pass?"

"Oh, I enjoy that as much as the next guy. I just think it's fun to understand why something is happening, too. In this case, physics explains why the ball spins in a spiral, but an-

A perfect spiral sends the ball spinning directly to its target.

other science can be used to look at why that spiral pattern is more efficient in the air."

"Great," Gordo groaned. "More science. Is it time to leave for the stadium yet?"

"Soon," Buck answered. "But first I want to talk about **aerodynamics**."

"Wait, now we're in outer space? How did we get there?" Gordo said, throwing up his hands.

"What are you talking about?" Buck said, and then understood. "Right, okay, no, aerodynamics is not about rockets, it's about the study of any object in flight. In this case, it's a football moving with a spiral motion. In aerodynamics, scientists study **drag**, which is what we might call air resistance or wind resistance. Drag is what slows down an object moving through the air. Combine that with gravity, which is pulling toward the Earth, and you've got a football that has to land somewhere . . . some time."

"Well, if the quarterback does his job, that's right in my hands!" Gordo said and pretended to spike the football he was holding.

"It lands there because the spiral creates the best shape to reduce drag. A wobbling ball has a wider surface facing into the air that causes higher drag. More drag, less speed."

"Congratulations, Buck, you've just proved what football players have always known," said Gordo, laughing. "The best pass is the one that reaches its target!"

Pigskin Tales

Footballs have created a variety of legends over the years, from what they are made from to what they can do to how far they can be thrown.

• It's not true that footballs are made from pigskin. They got that mistaken nickname because early footballs were much rounder and shaped somewhat like the body of a pig! All footballs today are made of cowhide leather.

• The great Denver Broncos quarterback John Elway was one of the most power-packed passers the game has ever seen. In his prime, he threw the football so hard that if a receiver missed the ball and it hit his chest, the ball left a mark. The X made by the point of the ball came to be known as The Elway Cross.

• Some fun facts about the official Wilson NFL football: About ten balls can be made from a typical cowhide; the Ohio factory makes about 700,000 footballs each year; the "K" on the NFL ball means it is only used by kickers and held by officials until a kicking play is called.

Try It Yourself!

Tune up your arm! It's time to throw! In this activity, you'll have to be able to throw with a spiral. If you can't, or if you know someone who is a good football player, go ahead and recruit them. Scientists bring in test subjects all the time. You can also use an experienced passer and an inexperienced one to compare their results.

Suggested Materials:
- football (preferably a good leather one)
- football player, either good or inexperienced
- something to act as targets—papers on an outside wall, a cone hanging from a tree, or a person holding a cardboard target (away from their face!)
- paper and pencil to keep track of passes and results
- stopwatch

As Buck and Gordo discussed, a spiral will make a football fly straighter and faster. This experiment will try to prove that.

1. Set up your targets about 10 yards from the passer.

2. Have them throw the football with the best spiral they can at the target.

3. For good spirals that hit the target, record the time the pass took as well as how near the target the throw was. Discount any passes that wobble too much (those are for later).

4. Repeat the spiral throwing at a farther distance, say, 25 yards. Record times and nearness to the targets.

5. Now go back to 10 yards and throw without a spiral. Try to make the passes wobble, or even have them thrown end over end. Time these passes, too.

6. Which moved faster? Yes, your eyes can tell you the spirals probably did but now you have the data. At the longer distance, can a poorly spiraling ball even reach the target? How much longer does such a throw take to arrive?

4
THE POWER
OF POWER

Buck moved on to a display of football helmets. "You always keep yours pumped up, right, buddy?" he said to Gordo.

"Heck, yes, man," Gordo said. "I might not be as smart as you are, but I know that keeping my head protected is number one on the field."

Buck was referring to the internal air pockets that come in most football helmets. Inflated with air after the helmet is put on the player's head, the pockets compress when struck or hit. By absorbing some of the force of the blow, the pockets lessen the amount of force that ends up affecting the player. The same concept works in the padding worn on the players' bodies. By absorbing force, the padding reduces its impact on bodies.

"I'm glad to hear you say that, Gordo," Buck said seriously. "I worry about you out there. I know it's fun, but you can really get hurt."

"Yeah, I know," Gordo said. "We all know. And we try to tackle the right way and not go for head shots. But we love the game so much that we just try to put up with the pain and deal with injuries as they come."

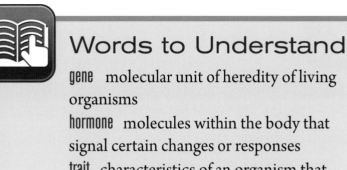

Words to Understand

gene molecular unit of heredity of living organisms

hormone molecules within the body that signal certain changes or responses

trait characteristics of an organism that are inherited from the passing of genetic material from parent to offspring

"Have you read the reports about how the NFL and college football are working to reduce the number of concussions? That's a good step in the right direction, of course. What do you know about the science of getting smacked?" Buck asked.

"There you go with science again," snorted Gordo. "I know it hurts. And it hurts less if you've got the right pads."

"I hate to throw a little math into the discussion, but the impact of a guy tackling you can be written down this way: $F = ma$. The m is the mass, or weight of the guy doing the hitting. The a is the acceleration, or speed he's moving at. Multiply them and you get F, which is the amount of force that's hitting you. A heavier guy will create more force, but so will a faster guy. Increase both and you've got a very heavy force."

"Don't I know it," Gordo said. "I'd rather get hit by a little guy than a big guy. Thank you, science!"

"I'll let science know your appreciation," Buck laughed. "That equation explains why there are fewer injuries when little kids play. They are all mostly the same size and they can't move as fast. When they get older and faster, and they are not all roughly the same weight, that's when too much force can be applied."

"So if I'm wearing a big helmet and it's all pumped up, how come my head can still hurt after I get knocked around?" Gordo asked.

"That's because of what happens in a concussion. It's not the action of the blow, it's the reaction of your brain in your skull. When you get hit in the front, for example, your brain actually sloshes inside your skull, whacking the inside back. So a blow to the front can give you a concussion in the back of your brain. Of course, it might hurt in front, too, but that's damage to the skin or bone, not the brain."

"Well, I'm still going to keep playing, Gordo said. "But I will definitely be careful out there."

Is Football Dying?

He got dinged. He got his bell rung. He got knocked dizzy. Football players have long had a number of ways to avoid saying that a player has suffered a concussion. The culture of the game led players to often laugh off symptoms. In recent years, however, the laughing has stopped. Numerous studies have shown the long-term dangers

of repeated blows to the head. Players such as Hall of Famer Troy Aikman (above) have seen their careers cut short. Others have seen their lives shortened. Tragic suicides linked to concussion syndrome and a call from fans and players alike have led to rules changes to try to limit head-to-head hits. Medical officials are now more empowered to pull players from games. Equipment makers are seeking more protective and safer helmets. With all this effort, however, some people think that football is in long-term danger as more and more young people look at the long-term risks compared to the relatively small potential for great success.

Try It Yourself!

Can you make protective padding that works as well as the pros? Instead of risking your head and your bones, in this activity, you'll risk an egg. The idea is to use creativity and design to build a protective cage or case for an egg . . . and then drop it. Will the egg survive? We provided a list of supplies, but what other supplies could you add to the list that could improve your design? Remember, engineers designing pads for athletes have to blend the function of protection with form; in other words, what are they made of and what do they look like? Football players can't play inside a tank, though that would give them more protection. It's a balancing act.

Materials:
- eggs
- plastic wrap
- pieces of cardboard of various sizes
- packing tape
- packing peanuts
- tissue paper

1. Pick an egg that you are going to protect.

2. Set up the parameters of your experiment. How big will you allow the egg case to be? Try it once without limits, and then see how much you can pare it down. What's the smallest case you can make?

3. Build the case around the egg. Try out different combinations of the protective products.

4. Does more tissue paper help? How can you use the peanuts? What should go on the outside, something soft or something hard?

5. When you think you've created the best version of your egg case, it's time to test it.

6. Drop the egg from a safe place that is at least 12-15 feet (3.6–4.5 m) high, such as a second-story window or over the edge of a staircase. (Hint: It's a good idea to do this drop outside; science can be messy, especially when using eggs.)

7. Did the egg survive? Good science sometimes means breaking a lot of eggs, so if it didn't make it, keep trying for the best and most successful designs.

5
DIMPLES
ON THE GREEN

"**N**ow here's a sport where you don't have to protect your head," Gordo said, advancing toward the golf section of the store.

"Not unless you're standing near the golf course when you're playing," laughed Buck. "If I was watching you, I'd wear a helmet!"

"Hey, you're no Tiger Woods, either, hacker," Gordo said. The guys often took time out on weekends to knock golf balls around a small course near their house. Neither was a star, but it was a fun way to get outdoors and to work on a new skill.

Buck moved to a basket of golf balls on display. He picked one up and showed it to Gordo.

"You know how we talked about drag when we were looking at the footballs?" he asked. "Science has a lot to do with how golf balls move through the air, too."

"Is there an app that will make me hit it straighter?" Gordo asked. "Or do you have an experiment that will teach me to nail every putt?"

"No," Buck laughed. "Those are up to you! But the design of a golf ball does help golfers who know what they're doing hit it farther."

Buck had seen a documentary about early golf, and since his father was a big golf fan, had been to golf shows to see new gear. Along the way, he had picked up a lot of interesting trivia about the bumpy little balls.

"The first golf balls were completely smooth," he said. "Some were even made of wood. But as the early golfers knocked the balls around, the balls got nicked or cut. The golfers found that the scratched balls went farther and straighter than the smooth ones."

"Well, that's not what you said about drag and footballs," Gordo pointed out. "Wouldn't a smooth ball have less air resistance, since there's nothing blocking the air or the wind as it passes over the ball? Got you there, Einstein!"

"Normally, yes, something that is smoother will move through the air better," Buck answered. "But we've got other forces at work here. Air moving over a surface, especially a rounded surface like this, has two types of flow. Air moves over a smooth surface in a laminar flow.

The impact of the clubhead on the ball provides the force to send it into the air.

Tennis Fuzz, Anyone?

While golfers want a hard ball that will fly smoothly through the air, as well as one that will bounce and roll well, tennis players are actually hoping things slow down. A tennis ball without the fuzz on the outside would move so quickly it might be impossible to see, let alone return. The fuzz on the outside acts as an air brake, creating resistance to the power put on the ball by the player's racquet. The fuzz also slightly deadens the bounce, or compression, of the ball as it hits the ground, creating a true and level path. Of course, the top players can still make that fuzzy ball move pretty fast. Serves on the men's pro tour routinely top 125 miles (200 km) per hour.

That air quickly separates from the object, but behind the object, a **vortex** is created by the swirling air. That vortex actually creates more drag. However, if you put bumps or cuts or scratches on the object, you get a turbulent flow. That sticks to the ball better, reduces the vortex, and allows for longer flight."

"So why don't golfers just experiment and make all sorts of cuts and bumps on the ball to create more of that turbulence?" asked Gordo, seeing a way to cut down on his bad shots.

"Actually, they do," Buck answered. "Golf ball makers spend millions of dollars each year on wind-tunnel testing, computer modeling, and simulations to try to find a pattern of dimples—that's what they call the little indentations—that will work better than what is out there now. It's a huge industry, all based on aerodynamic science."

"Let me at that display," Gordo said. "I'm going to try every pattern they have until I find one that can cure my slice."

"Dude, I'm afraid the golf ball is not your problem there," laughed Buck. "For that, you have to look in the mirror!"

Try It Yourself

The way that air flows over a golf ball affects its flight. In this activity, you can "see" how air flows over a variety of shapes. There is no right answer for this one, but it's a great demonstration of the principles of aerodynamics.

Materials:
- hair dryer (use on cool setting!)
- ribbons of varying lengths
- tape
- cans, boxes, tubes, and balls of varying sizes and shapes

1. Tape two ribbons of equal length to the top and bottom of the hair dryer at the place where air exits the nozzle.

2. Turn on the hair dryer to the cool setting. The ribbons should flutter out in front of the dryer nozzle.

3. Hold some of the tubes or balls in front of the airflow from the nozzle, between the ribbons. Observe how the ribbons curve to form over the ball. Can you see how the airflow changes when it has to go around an object? (Keep your hand or fingers behind the object so you don't affect the airflow.)

4. Now try the same with boxes or cans. How are the patterns of airflow different? If you were designing something that had to move through the air—a car, a plane, a truck—how would you change the design now that you can see how air flows over different shapes?

6

HIGH CURVES AT HIGH SPEED

A loud sound from nearby made the guys turn their heads quickly. It sounded like cars crashing, but they were in a store.

"Up there," Gordo pointed, "on the TV screen. They're showing highlights from a stock car race from this past weekend."

The crash was happening in slow-motion now, as the video replayed it. One of the cars was driving at high speed around a corner of the track, when it suddenly slid violently to the outside and crashed into the wall. Several other cars coming behind it could not stop or swerve and hit the wrecked car. It was like a demolition derby.

"Man, I wish our physics teacher was here to see that," Buck said. "I know what he'd say.

'Those drivers might be fast, but they didn't study their physics!'"

"Okay, now I think you're making stuff up," Gordo said. "Racing cars is just seeing who goes the fastest. The only science there is how hard you can step on the gas pedal."

"Might this be a reason you haven't passed your driving test yet," Buck asked.

"Hey, that's not fair," Gordo protested. "My mom's station wagon doesn't work right."

As his friend continued to protest, Buck remembered what the physics teacher had said about the forces acting on moving objects. The teacher had shown them something called **centrifugal force**, which pushes objects moving around a point away from the center of the point. But that's not what is happening here, he thought.

"Gordo," he began, "seriously, without physics none of those cars could go anywhere near that fast. We learned about something called **centripetal force**, which is different than the spinning centrifugal force you might be familiar with."

"Yes, that one I remember," Gordo said. "I'm still trying to get the yo-yo down from the tree. I was spinning it around and around and it slipped off my finger and man, that thing flew! Wait, is that what happened to the car in that wreck?"

"Actually, no, that was the loss of centripetal force," Buck said. "As the cars whip around the track, the bank or tilt of the track is actually forcing them inward via centripetal force. It takes their skill and those powerful engines to counteract that and keep the cars going forward."

The wings and spoiler on this car create downforce to help the driver.

Ready . . . Set . . . Go Really Fast!

While NASCAR and IndyCar vehicles can hit pretty good speeds, they have to slow down around corners and even stop in the pits. Their races take hours and demand intense fitness from both their drivers and their engines. The sport of drag racing, however, is a different kind of speed all together. In a drag race, a pair of cars (or motorcycles) wait side-by-side for a green light. The cars then accelerate at a tremendous speed, reaching more than 300 miles (482 km) per hour in just 1,000 feet (91.4 m). Races are over in seconds. How do these cars generate that much thrust and force? Huge engines are a big part of the story. A Top Fuel dragster puts out more than 7,000 horsepower. Compare that to a standard family car of perhaps 200 hp, or even a NASCAR engine that can top 700 or so. In addition, the Top Fuel cars are very light, more than 60 percent lighter than a regular passenger car. Combine the force of that powerful engine with the reduced mass of the vehicle and you've got an equation for some serious speed.

"That's not what I thought was happening," Gordo said. "That's pretty cool. So those tilted tracks actually help the drivers maintain speed and control."

"That's the plan," Buck said. "Those stock cars also have to deal with drag, just like we saw with footballs and golf balls. But in other kinds of racing, drag is counteracted by the design of the race cars themselves. In fact, without some of the features on the open-wheel racers, cars might fly."

"Now that I'd pay to see!" Gordo said.

"Well . . . it actually would be really dangerous," Buck said. "To avoid that danger, the open-wheel racers in IndyCar and Formula 1 have wings that push air easily and quickly over the cars, and spoilers in the back, too. As the air rushes over them, it actually pushes the cars toward the track, creating what is called **downforce**. Drivers learn they can keep their speed up through some turns thanks to the downforce."

"Now I know how I can pass my driver's test," Gordo said. "Put wings on mom's car!"

Try It Yourself

Want to see centripetal force in action? You don't have to drive a race car or even travel to Daytona. You can see the effect that this force has on those race cars, but in this activity you might get a little wet.

Materials:
- a bucket (plastic, so it's lighter weight)
- heavy string or rope
- water

1. Tie the rope to the handle of the bucket
2. Fill the bucket about a third full of water.
3. Make sure and do this experiment outside, where you can spill water without making anyone mad.
4. Slowly start to twirl the bucket around you, using the rope. Start low to the ground and slowly raise the level of the spin until it is horizontal to the ground. What happens to the water?
5. Try to spin faster and faster. What does the water do now?
6. For a further experiment, see if you can spin the bucket fast enough in the vertical plane (that is, so it is upside down above you during the spin) without spilling the water.
7. Centripetal force should keep the water in the bucket if you spin fast enough.
8. Try some variations by seeing how full you can make the bucket and still keep the water in. How long can you make the rope and still create enough force to keep the water in? Physics can be fun . . . and wet.

7
REPLACEMENT PARTS

The guys finally headed toward the racks of clothing that Buck wanted to check out for his new running clothes. On their way there, they watched another man come toward them. He walked with a slight limp and as he passed, both Buck and Gordo saw that the man had an artificial left leg from the knee down.

"Man, that would be tough," Gordo sighed. "I can't imagine losing a leg and not being able to run anymore."

"That's not true anymore, of course," Buck said. "With advances in science and engineering, people can run nearly as fast with artificial legs as real ones. Some of the runners in the Paralympic Games can nearly reach Olympic-caliber speed. And they're certainly faster than you are!"

"Hey, easy there, Lightning," Gordo said, pushing his friend good-naturedly, "you're not exactly the Flash, either."

"Regardless of our speed," Buck continued, "it really is amazing what can be done with prosthetics these days."

"I thought we were talking about legs, not teeth," Gordo said.

"Prosthetics, not orthodontics," Buck said. "Biologists have learned a lot about the human body and how it moves. Engineers are using lighter materials to make the prosthetics easier to use and to fit better. Even computer engineers are merging that technology with the limbs so that some can now be controlled directly by the person's brain power."

"Wow, that's amazing," Gordo said. "How do they do that?"

"By connecting electrical circuits to the remaining nerve endings, and then retraining the brain through practice to send signals down that pathway, some patients can move prosthetic fingers to pick things up. It's been amazing for some of our veterans who were seriously wounded in Iraq or Afghanistan."

"But what about the running you mentioned?" Gordo asked.

"One of the most well-known inventions is called the Flex-Foot. An American engineer named Van Phillips created it. Instead of looking like a real foot, the Flex-Foot looks like the letter C. That gives it a way to be sort of springy. After a person learns to move while wearing one or even two of these devices, they can really run well. It takes a different kind of balance, but the stride of the runner is just about the same.

"The other big improvement, along with designs like that, is what the prosthetics are made from. Older models used steel or aluminum along with plastics. They were fine, but with the use of lightweight but very strong stuff like carbon fiber, prosthetics have really come a long way."

"Can they run faster than they could when they had legs?" Gordo wondered. "Couldn't having space age parts give you an advantage? I mean, I'm not saying it's worth losing your legs, but you did say they were faster than me!"

"A turtle is faster than you," teased Buck. "But seriously, you bring up a point. Some athletes have tried to earn spots racing against athletes without prostheses. Some of those athletes objected and said that the springy feet did provide an advantage. It's only happened a couple of times, but the officials decided to let the runners with prosthetics take part."

Olympics for All

Prosthetics and other scientific and engineering advances help physically disabled athletes continue to compete. The biggest world competition for these athletes is the Paralympics. The first Paralympics was held in Rome in 1960. The event grew out of competitions held in England following World War II that were created to give men injured during the war a way to stay active. The worldwide movement grew from the Rome event to become a competition held every four years to coincide with the Summer and Winter Olympic Games. In dozens of sports, including sled hockey (right), athletes use engineering adaptations to help them use their physical and mental skills to earn medals and honor for themselves and their countries.

"Still," said Gordo, "I'm sure they'd probably prefer not to have to worry about whether their prosthetic limbs helped or not. They'd probably rather not have been injured."

"Plus, scientists are coming up with new ideas all the time," added Buck. "I just read about one experiment that is trying to connect artificial eyes with people's brains to help them see again."

"Perfect," Gordo said. "Then they can watch the Paralympics on TV!"

Try It Yourself

Though science has made great strides in helping people with missing limbs, it has not solved all the problems. Living with a missing limb is a challenge, even with the use of these high-tech replacements. For this activity, it's time to put yourself in their place. You'll arrange to spend a little time without the use of one or another limb and see how you'd react and how your daily life might be different.

Materials:
- a plastic bag and a rubber band
- a mitten or a glove
- a large rubber band or a long cloth for tying
- an eye patch
- crutches or a cane

1. Start by "taking away" a thumb. Use the rubber band or cloth to tie your thumb to your palm. Then try to do a few things with only one thumb. Can you tie your shoes? Can you open a jar? Can you read a book? What about buttoning a shirt? What adaptations do people with only one thumb have to make? How would these adaptations change if you try "losing" both thumbs?

2. To see what life with one hand might be like, put the mitten over a fist so your fingers can't be used. Or tie the plastic bag over your fist. (Don't leave rubber bands on your hands for very long and don't make them so tight that they make your hands or fingers numb.) Then try some of the same sort of activities. How does having one hand make those things harder? How do you have to adapt your motions and actions with just one hand?

3. Perform a similar set of experiments wearing the eye patch. How is your vision affected? What things are harder with just one eye? (Please don't drive or ride your bike with the eye patch on.)

4. For a real challenge, bend your leg up behind you and tie it there for a few minutes. Using the cane or crutches . . . or not . . . briefly experience life with one leg. Having firsthand experiences like these give us new respect for the people who live with these situations every day.

8

TO SWEAT OR
NOT TO SWEAT

"Finally," Gordo huffed. "Can we pick up your fancy new running gear and get back to campus? If I'm not there on time, I'll be riding the pine the whole game."

"No worries," Buck said. "Here we are."

He stopped in front of a colorful display of shorts, shirts, socks, and more. A big poster of an Olympic track star hung above the display.

"There is so much to choose from," Buck said admiringly. "What we wear to work out and play in has come a long way. It's not just a cotton T-shirt and gym shorts anymore."

"You've got that right," said a voice. A young woman wearing a name badge that said "Annie" approached them. "Can I help you find what you're looking for?"

"That would be great," Buck said. "One thing I know I need is something that will keep me comfortable even when I'm sweating a lot."

"We have several types of shirts and shorts that can help with that. Engineers and scientists have been creating fabrics that **wick** the sweat away from your body, instead of just absorbing it into the material.

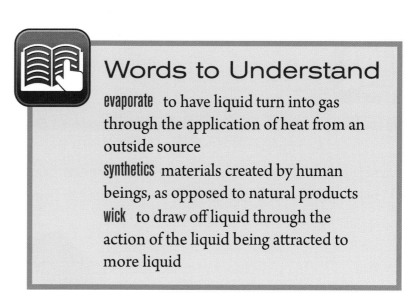

Then by letting the moisture **evaporate** away from the fabric instead of holding it in, you actually get cooler. Evaporation drains the heat energy, so you cool off by sweating. And these high-tech fabrics keep you from getting too waterlogged!

"And if you don't like the feel of **synthetics**—some of them can be a little slippery—some of these shirts here are made of lightweight wool, a natural fiber. The wool has been changed, though, to be able to absorb moisture but still feel dry, while still allowing for evaporation.

"Did you have colors in mind?" Annie went on. "You probably have heard that white is a good color for running in the sun, because it reflects the sun's rays. Black shirts normally would feel hotter because they absorb that light. However, this new style of shirt is dark-colored, but the fabric is engineered to reflect just about any light. It's called 'coldblack' and is the latest thing to hit the market."

"That's very cool . . . literally!" Buck joked. "I've also read about compression products. What's the deal with those?"

"Scientists and doctors know that support can help most muscle groups perform more efficiently," Annie said. "But most of the wraps that are used by therapists were too binding and didn't move and stretch with the athlete. The new wraps, however, are made with a new fabric and a new weave that can stretch in any direction. You can wear comfortable, soft compression shorts or leggings to help support your muscles while you run. You can wear them alone or under other running gear."

"What about running shoes?" Annie asked. "Do you need to look at those, too? There have been some great advances in design. For instance, you can have your foot measured and a machine can create a tread pattern that works just for your foot using 3-D printing technology. And the uppers of some shoes are now made of almost airweight material. The Nike FlyKnit products are made of engineered yarn so that the shoes don't have seams that can rub against your

The Old Days

Do you own a wool sweater or coat? Feel how thick it is? Now imagine putting that sweater on, plus pants made of the same stuff, and playing baseball in the hot sun for three hours. Before the creation of modern synthetic jersey material, athletes in many sports were burdened with heavy, stuffy, sweat-absorbing material like wool and flannel. They often were also charged with washing their own uniforms. And in Major League contracts until the 1950s, players were issued two sets of uniforms for the entire season. If they did not return them clean and whole, the team charged them for replacement or repair! The material jerseys are made from is not the only thing that has changed over the years!

foot. They're also incredibly lightweight, but very strong."

"What is this, science fiction or sports?" Gordo asked.

"Hey, you football players can't have all the science in sports," Buck said. "Runners spend about three billion dollars a year on shoes in the United States. Every company is trying to make theirs the latest and greatest."

"Three billion dollars on sneakers!" exclaimed Gordo. "That's amazing!"

"Well, I'm going to add to that total," Buck said. "Let me have these in a size 10, plus two of the sweat-wicking shirts . . . in basic black! And then we've gotta go!"

Try It Yourself

You've got to sweat a little for this one. Don't worry . . . a little exercise is always a good thing. You can even choose the activity that gets you sweaty. Running? Walking? Lifting weights? Archery? Well, for that last one you might have to move pretty quickly picking up the arrows to get sweaty, but whatever works. The point is that you'll be comparing the efficiency of different kinds of fabric to see how they deal with sweat.

Suggested Materials:

- a cotton T-shirt (check the label)
- a T-shirt made from a synthetic fabric such as polyester or rayon
- an activity that makes you sweaty (see above)
- scale to weigh clothing, perhaps a kitchen scale

1. This might take a couple of days to complete. First measure and record the weight of the cotton T-shirt and the synthetic T-shirt.

2. On the first day, perform your sweat-inducing activity for 15 minutes while wearing the cotton T-shirt.

3. Remove the sweaty shirt and quickly weigh it. Record the difference from its dry weight.

4. On the second day, repeat the same activity for the same 15 minutes, this time wearing the synthetic shirt.

5. Remove the sweaty shirt and quickly weigh it. Record the difference from its dry weight.

6. What did you discover? Does cotton really soak up the sweat? Did the synthetic shirt also increase in weight? The answers might show you that the idea of sweat-wicking synthetic fibers is a pretty good one!

9
CONCLUSION

Sports Science. Sports, athletics, games, working out—whatever way that you take part in physical activity, science has always played a part, and emerging technologies are adding more and more ways every day.

The very actions of the body are described by biology and **biomechanics**. By understanding how the body takes in fuel, as in Chapter 1, you can better understand how to give your body the fuel to move. Scientists are always adding new information to the topic as well. For example, have you heard about **dynamic** stretching? Read up online about this new way to warm up for physical activity. Many top pros are adding this to their routines. Instead of **static** stretching, which is basically standing in one place and moving each muscle group in turn, dynamic stretching adds movement. That is, you move while stretching, you combine muscles so that they work together, and you mimic movements you'll do in the actual activity.

Scientists and physical therapists working with the United States Tennis Association, in the martial arts, and with national soccer organizations are all recommending this type of stretching. You can see videos online. Dynamic stretching is also a lot more fun than standing around doing toe touches.

Words to Understand

biomechanics the study of how the bodies of living things, usually humans, move
dynamic in motion, having movement, not standing still
static remaining in one place; not changing position

Biologists and doctors are also studying just how much activity a person should do, whether that is playing a sport or just getting up and moving. In fact, "sitting disease" is a growing problem among people who work in an office all day (or who sit around all night playing computer games). The latest studies are showing that even a small amount of moving around—not sitting—can pay off. Look at a stand up desk and see if it might work for you. In the office of the future, you might not have a choice!

In several places in the book, we talked about materials science. That is, the science of how things are made and what they are made from. Chemistry has played a big role in that process, creating synthetic materials that are stronger, lighter, and longer-lasting than natural materials. Tennis racquets are made of the same carbon fiber that have helped make safer cars. Aluminum bats in baseball are being replaced by durable plastics that act more like wooden bats, but don't break as easily. New types of artificial turf use recycled rubber from sneakers to provide a bouncy surface.

Chemistry has also been in the sports news in recent years for less positive reasons. Some athletes have chosen to use performance-enhancing drugs (PEDs) to change their bodies or to help them heal faster. Nearly every major sports organization bans

Tennis racquets are now made of lightweight but super-strong carbon fiber.

What comes up must come down, thanks to gravity.

most uses of these substances. They can cause great long-term harm to the person's body, though they can provide some short-term gain. Adding to the physical harm is the issue of fairness. Should some athletes be able to do things that others can't? Does that give them an unfair advantage? Sports is about fair competition. Everyone should be on the same level, and may the best athlete win. When athletes cheat using science, they cheat themselves and they misuse the science.

Like any tool that an athlete uses—the gear, the clothing, the gym, the arena, and their own internal desire—science should be put to its best and most positive use. Some areas of sports science happen on their own; physical forces affect the way the games are played just as they affect our every day life (imagine a pole vaulting competition without gravity, for instance!). Other areas of science are put into play by choice. It is in making the right choices of how to use science that people involved with sports show they are really winners—by ensuring that science is used to help all athletes, not just a few.

Sports Science 24–7: Concept Review

Chapter 1

Buck and Gordo learn about how good nutrition provides the fuel that any athlete needs, whether they are big-time pros or everyday high school players.

Chapter 2

Soccer fans and baseball fans thrill at what their heroes can do with the balls in their sports, but those players can thank physics for some of their success.

Chapter 3

To spiral or not to spiral, that is the question in football. The answer, as the guys find out, is that a spiral is faster, thanks to lower air resistance.

Chapter 4

The issue of impact injuries is very much part of the world sports conversation. In this section, Buck and Gordo learn about how science is trying to lessen those impacts.

Chapter 5

Smoother is faster, right? Not so fast! Buck and Gordo learn how those little bumps and dimples in golf balls are actually the keys to a sure flight.

Chapter 6

Gentlemen, start your physics! Buck and Gordo head to the virtual track to see how forces from science play a huge part in a race car's ability to reach top speeds.

Chapter 7

Engineers have transformed the lives of people around the world by creating prosthetic limbs. Some of those people have continued as top athletes as a result.

Chapter 8

Science doesn't stop at the field, it heads to the locker room, as new fabrics in clothing and new constructions of shoes have helped athletes perform better.

FIND OUT MORE

Books

Dig into the science of biology and how people and scientists are using it to tap into the potential of every person to improve.

McClusky, Mark. *Faster, Higher, Stronger: How Sports Science Is Creating a New Generation of Superathletes.* New York: Hudson Street Press, 2014.

We didn't have room for martial arts in this book, so you can read more about science and the fighting arts in this one.

Thalken, Jason. *Fight Like a Physicist: The Incredible Science Behind Martial Arts.* Wolfeboro, N.H.: YMAA Publishing, 2013.

Looking for your favorite sport? It's probably in here, a book that covers the science involved in more than a dozen sports.

Vizard, Frank (editor). *Why a Curveball Curves: The Incredible Science of Sports.* New York: Popular Mechanics Press, 2009.

Web Sites

Check out stories from sports science from the "world leader" in sports broadcasting.
espn.go.com/espn/sportscience/

The science museum Exploratorium in San Francisco has a long list of articles on aspects of sports science.
http://www.exploratorium.edu/taxonomy/term/36/0

Want to go deep? Check out this site, which has advanced looks and insights into sports science. For experts only!
sportsscientists.com/

SERIES GLOSSARY OF KEY TERMS

alleles   different forms of a gene; offspring inherit one allele from each parent

chromosomes   molecules within an organism which contain DNA

climate change   the ongoing process in which the temperature of the Earth is growing over time

force   in science, strength or energy that comes as a result of a physical movement or action

frequency   number of waves that pass a given point in a certain period of time

friction   the resistance encountered when an object rubs against another object or on a surface

gene   molecular unit of heredity of living organisms

gravity   the force that pulls objects toward the ground

greenhouse gases   gases in the atmosphere that trap radiation from the sun

inertia   tendency of an object to resist change in motion

laser   an intensified beam of light

lift   the force that acts to raise a wing or an airfoil

momentum   the amount of motion by a moving object

semiconductor a substance that has a conductivity between that of an insulator and that of most metals

sustainable   able to be maintained at a certain rate or level

traits   characteristics of an organism that are passed to the next generation

wavelength   a measurement of light that is the distance from the top of one wave to the next

Picture Credits

Baseball Hall of Fame: 14

Dollar Photo: Sparkia 16

Dreamstime.com
      Studio38 8
      Rblisset 12
      Aspenphoto 17
      Amaviael 24
      Photoinnovation 25
      Alexstar 26
      Actionsports 28
      Sergeibach 29
      Raytags 30
      Mezzotintdreamstime 32, 42
      Id1974 34
      Martinmark 36
      Bcnewell 38
      Razvanjp 40
      Stockman21 41

Newscom: Andrew Dieb Icon SMI 10; Todd Kirkland/Icon SMI 20; Tom Pennington/Fort Worth Star Telegram 22

ABOUT THE AUTHOR

Jane P. Gardner has written more than a dozen books for young and young-adult readers on science and other nonfiction topics. She became an author after a career as a science educator. She lives in Massachusetts with her husband, two sons, plus a cat and a gecko!

ABOUT THE CONSULTANT

Russ Lewin has taught physics, robotics, astronomy, and math at Santa Barbara Middle School in California for more than 25 years. His creative and popular classes and curriculum include a hands-on approach to learning and exploring that instills a love of science in his students.

INDEX